Civil War Dogs
and the
Men Who Loved Them

Anne Palagruto

To
Fiona & Ian

THE DOG OF THE REGIMENT

Author Unknown

If I were a poet like you my friend,
Said a bronzed old sergeant speaking to me,
I would make a rhyme of this mastiff here,
For a right good Union dog is he.
Although he was born on secesh soil
 And his master fought in the rebel ranks
If you'll do it I'll tell you his history
And give you in pay why a soldier's thanks.
Well the way we came across him was this,
We were on the march and twas getting late,
When we reached a farm house deserted by all,
Save this mastiff here who stood at the gate.
Thin and gaunt as a wolf was he,
And a piteous whine he gave twixt the bars,
But bless you if he didn't jump for joy,
When he saw our flag with the Stripes and Stars
Next day when we started again on the march,
With us went Jack without word or call,
Stopping for rest at the order to halt,
And taking his rations along with us all.
Never straggling but keeping his place in line,
Far to the right and close beside me,
And I don't care where the other is found,
There never was better drilled dog than he
He always went with us into the fight,
And the thicker the bullets fell around,
And the louder the rattling musketry rolled,
Louder and fiercer his bark would sound
And once when wounded and left for dead'
After a bloody and desperate fight'
Poor Jack as faithful as friend can be,
Lay by my side on the field all night.
And so when our regiment home returned,
We brought him along with us as you see,
And Jack and I being much attached,
The boys seemed to think he belonged to me.
And here he has lived with me ever since,
Right pleased with his quarters too he seems,
There are no more battles for brave old Jack,
And no more marches except in dreams.
But the best of all times for the old dog is,
When the thunder mutters along the sky,
Then he wakes the echoes around with his bark,
Thinking the enemy surely is nigh.
Now I've told you his history wrote him a rhyme,
Some day poor Jack in his grave must rest,
And of all the rhymes of this cruel war,
Which your brain has made let his be the best.

From The Rebellion Record; A Diary of American Events
By Frank Moore, 1865

Contents

1
Why Dogs?

As early as 1500 B.C. man began to write about his dog. There are drawings of dogs in the tombs of the ancient kings of Egypt, in the ruins of Pompeii, in the tapestries of medieval France and England and on the pottery of American Indians. All through Greek and Roman history the dog is mentioned as man's hunter, shepherd, watchdog or warrior. The Ethiopians actually elected a dog their King.

The first wild dogs made their appearance in North America about fifteen million years ago. Some scientists believe that the earliest wild dog was actually a mix between a wolf and a jackal, and that these puppies were the very first wild animals that man ever tamed. Although dogs as well as men were hunters, when a man killed his prey he didn't use the whole animal. Dogs were attracted to human villages because bones and bits of flesh were usually easy to find there. Dogs of the past learned that by hanging around the places men lived, they could grab a quick bite to eat without having to hunt.

At this point in time, man lived a very dangerous life. Large carnivorous animals were everywhere and hostile neighboring tribes could invade at any time, so early humans took advantage of these scavengers, the wild dogs, hanging around their homes. After a while the dogs, who frequently visited a village for food, began to see the village as their own territory. Whenever a strange human or wild beast approached, the dogs would bark ferociously, alerting villagers in time to rally some sort of defense if needed. As long as dogs were present, the human guards did not need to be as vigilant, allowing for more rest and a better lifestyle.

Many years later, in the 1600s, European settlers carried their own kinds of dogs to the New World. These dogs were hunters, guardians, herders, and also companions. Beginning in the 1800s, Americans began to value pets as companions and associated

Bartolomé Esteban Perez Murillo 1645-1650

them with happy family life, social status, and leisure. 19th century Americans believed that kindness to animals was part of good character. They felt that the experience of caring for pets taught children to be kind to others. Popular advice books for parents encouraged them to let their children care for animals, and families seemed to take this advice seriously. By the 1820s, many people believed that childhood cruelty to animals would lead to adult cruelty to people; therefore encouraging kindness became an important part of raising children. Sunday-school lessons, children's books, prints, and other objects all reinforced the importance of kindness. As a result, both rich and poor Americans chose to give dogs the status of "pet," and having pets became part of the ideal American childhood.

In the 20th century, many Americans treated their dogs as family at holiday celebrations, even buying them Christmas and birthday gifts. They began paying for or painting their own portraits of their pets. They also spent a lot of time playing with their pets, teaching them tricks and improvising or purchasing toys just for them. They gave their pets proper burials at home; and by the 1900s some people even paid for plots in pet cemeteries. Dogs

especially were entitled to good care for several reasons. First, they had the ability to feel pain and to suffer, just like people. Second, they seemed to have the good qualities that people needed: faithfulness and the ability to love unconditionally. Leslie Burgard, a certified pet dog trainer in State College, PA, said, "Their loyalty is unconditional, much like that between a parent and child. For the most part, our dogs would go to bat for us, even on our worst and most

1909 Postcard

intolerable day. All parents have days when they may not really like their kid that much, but they always love them unconditionally; even parents of troubled or criminal children love them on some level. The love and the loyalty that drives that emotion is instinctual...I think dogs have a 'love' or connection with their humans that is free of preconceived perceptions." By the 20th century, advocates of kindness to animals used four metaphors to compare dogs to people: dogs are loyal servants, dogs are loving parents, dogs are innocent like children, and dogs are true friends.

2
Dogs in the Civil War

So it seems dogs really ARE just like people, and this was certainly true of the dogs that accompanied the soldiers during the Civil War. They were important to the men for the companionship they provided, as well as the antics they performed. The morale of the men was always higher in regiments which had pets. The soldiers enjoyed playing with the animals and were eager to bestow upon their mascots larger-than-life attributes. Dogs became as much attached to army life as the soldiers were. They learned not to fear the thunder of the artillery and they chewed hard tack like veterans. Some dogs walked in line with their masters, some were mounted onto wagons or cannons, and others were carried in haversacks. Some even accompanied their masters to the front lines running back and forth fiercely barking at the enemy. Even the lowliest stray dog would become a regimental legend.

Old Abe and 8th Wisconsin Color Guard
Taken Soon after the Fall of Vicksburg

Although it was technically against orders to keep pets, soldiers kept dogs, cats, squirrels, raccoons, and other wildlife. One regiment from Wisconsin even had a pet eagle that was carried on its own perch next to the regimental flags. Nearly every regiment had a pet of some kind or other. Officers often overlooked the presence of a dog with a master in camp or on the march. Most of the soldiers had never been away from home before and many were very young. The officers felt that the dedication and friendship of these dogs helped ease the homesickness from which many of the soldiers suffered. Also, dogs allowed the soldiers a way to express affection and tenderness under terrible circumstances. Sgt. Martin Cross, 1st Virginia Artillery wrote "It mattered not whether the object of their affection was a dog, cat, possum, cow, or horse of whatever name or species, the brute was loved by all and woe be to the outsider who dared to insult or injure one of these pets."

Not surprisingly, dogs were the most popular mascots. Some dogs were picked up along the way but most were brought from home by the soldiers. The 35th Ohio Infantry had several dogs and the 34th Massachusetts Infantry had an "army of dogs". Some of the 34th's dogs were no more than wild animals always staying out of camp until dark and then sneaking in to the cook house when no one was near. Others became tame and would regularly fall in with the company. Some dogs went into the thick of battle growling and barking.

Before donning a gray uniform, Lieutenant Colonel Robert E. Lee once crossed the "Narrows" between Fort Hamilton and Staten Island, New York. Halfway over the body of water, he spied a dog with its head barely above the waves. He rescued the animal and named her Dart. He said in a letter to his wife, Dart went with him to his office every morning and lay down "from eight to four without moving." Dogs were also popular aboard vessels of war. John E. Pickle, of the *USS Fernandina,* who often went hunting ashore with excellent results, was accompanied by his two dogs, named 'Black' and 'Yellow.'

Jack, a black-and-white bull terrier who was present at nearly all the 102nd PA Infantry's battles in Virginia and Maryland, was a firehouse dog who joined the regiment along with the firemen. Major, a lion-hearted mutt who accompanied the 10th Maine, demonstrated his courage by snapping at Confederate Minie balls in flight. Unfortunately he caught one at Sabine Crossroads during the Red River Campaign in 1864 and perished. Frank, the mascot of the 2nd Kentucky Infantry, always accompanied his men into battle carrying his own small haversack around his neck with his own rations. When his company was captured Frank was incarcerated along with them at Fort Donelson in Tennessee. He spent six months in prison and when they were exchanged so was he. He stayed with the 2nd for two more years and then he came up missing and was presumed killed in action.

Dot was a little white spaniel who messed with a battery and was regarded as belonging to an Illinois regiment though his name might not be on the muster roll. He was under fire and twice wounded, leaving the tip of his tail at the battle of Stone River. The boys in the regiment washed the dog's silky white coat every day. They needed to do it because when the battery was on the march they just plopped Dot into the bucket with the cover on so they wouldn't lose him. The sponge bucket, swinging under the rear axle of the gun carriage, is not the tidiest chamber imaginable. One day the battery crossed a stream and the water came well up to the guns. Nobody remembered to check on Dot and when everyone was across the stream a gunner looked into the bucket and it was full of water. Poor little Dot had drowned.

The dog of the 5th Connecticut Infantry took a liking to officers and would seek out whoever was in command. This dog, a black and tan terrier, kept close to the captain or sergeant. On dress parades he left the company and went to the colonel and watched the parade pass. Many dogs were killed in action; however, this dog stayed with the officers and survived the war.

A Federal officer once brought a dog up from City Point, Virginia to Washington. He was an ugly looking dog but was a great pet with both the Union and Confederate pickets in front of Hancock's corps The dog had been trained to carry messages from time to time between the CSA and US pickets. A southern paper would be placed in his mouth and he would scamper off to the union lines, deliver up the paper and then return with a northern paper. He would at times be entrusted with packages of coffee and tobacco, which he always delivered promptly and safely. The Confederates; however, after a while used him for transmitting information from one portion of their lines to another and the four-legged messenger was caught with one of these contraband messages. The dog had to suffer a penalty for being disloyal, so he was confiscated and brought north.

Tony, the Newfoundland of the Chicago Light Artillery Battery A, was called the "battery dog". He was a dog of action and had no fear of the bullets zipping all around him. He was on the battlefield at South Mountain and then wounded at Fort Donelson. He saw action again at Shiloh. He never got separated from his men so when he came up missing at

Antietam the worst was feared. Unfortunately, he was killed and found beside the body of W. J. Pollock, Co H., 20th New York Infantry.

3
Jack, 102nd Pennsylvania Infantry

The 102nd Pennsylvania Infantry was made up mainly of volunteer firemen. Their mascot, a brown and white bull terrier named Union Jack, is one of the better-known dogs of the civil war. Jack wandered into the Fifth Avenue Fire House in Pittsburgh and became the firehouse dog. When the firefighters volunteered to join the 102nd, Jack, along with the men, became part of the regiment. After a few weeks Jack understood all the bugle calls and obeyed only the men of "his" regiment. His manners were very gentle, and even timid among his friends, but he was suspicious and fierce as a lion when among his enemies. Harpers Weekly published several stories about Jack throughout the war. The following is taken from one of those stories.

"But one of the most remarkable features in his character is his utter hatred of the rebels. His actions, in this respect, really seemed to go beyond brute instinct. No kindness, no attempt at caressing could get the "gray-coats" to win him over or even induce him to take food from them; but he growled and snapped at them upon all occasions, until many threatened to shoot him. When they got to the Richmond prison, another large dog was there being fondled by a secesh officer, and Jack stood looking at both, apparently with the greatest hatred and disgust. When the officer left, the secesh dog tried to scrape an acquaintance with Jack, but the latter did not covet any such friendship. He rushed upon the canine rebel, gave him a sound thrashing, and, although larger than himself, fairly tossed him over his head."

On the road, when dehydrated men were fainting from thirst, Jack would always run forward, and whenever he discovered a pool of water would rush back, barking loudly, to tell them. When they were supplied with only five crackers to each man for five days, with no meat, and the men were literally dying from starvation, Jack would go and catch chickens for them. He would intercept every rebel horse or wagon passing with food, and bark begging for them to bring relief. On one occasion, when a sick and exhausted Union soldier had been left behind, Jack stayed with him for several hours until a wagon picked him up. After a battle, Jack would fearlessly search the field for the dead and wounded of his regiment. Some of the battles included were the Wilderness campaigns, Spotsylvania, and the siege of Petersburg.

According to a regimental historian, Jack was wounded at the battle of Malvern Hill, but recovered and was captured by the Confederates at Savage's Station. Somehow, he escaped from prison. Jack survived the battle of Antietam on Sept. 17, 1862, the bloodiest day of the war, in which over 23,000 were killed, missing or wounded. Three months later he was wounded again at Fredericksburg, this time almost fatally. His comrades successfully nursed him back to health. At Salem Church, during the Chancellorsville Campaign, he was once again taken prisoner by the Confederates. After six months as a POW at Belle Isle, he was exchanged according to wartime protocol, one Yankee prisoner traded for one Confederate prisoner. After being exchanged Col. John Williams Patterson wrote on May 25th 1863, "I arrived here this morning from Richmond, where I have been a prisoner since the 4th. I passed through the fight at Fredericksburg unharmed. It was the hottest battle I have ever witnessed. I was taken on May the 4th at 10 O'clock PM after the army had retired. We were "gobbled" I suppose. I would not leave the post where stationed and when the Rebs came they had an easy fray. I tried to get away but could not...94 men, including Jack our dog were brought in...."

Jack rejoined his regiment and stayed with them through the Battle of the Wilderness and Spotsylvania campaigns and the siege of Petersburg. Jack's regiment was so grateful for his service and companionship that they collected enough money to purchase a beautiful silver collar, worth $75, which they ceremoniously presented to their canine friend in tribute to Jack's indomitable spirit and scrappy character. On the evening of Dec. 23, 1864, while his regiment was on furlough at Frederick, MD, Jack disappeared. Although the men looked all over for their mascot; and even offered a substantial reward, he had simply vanished, and was never seen or heard from again. It could be that Jack was stolen or murdered for his new silver collar, or he succumbed to a bullet, poison, or a trap... or just simply passed away-- his silver collar waiting to be dug up by a lucky artifact hunter.

4
Harvey, 104th Ohio Infantry

The 104th was started in Wellsville, Ohio and according to the regimental historian "an undue proportion of 'toughs' and 'deadbeats'" made up Company F as well as "Harvey and at least one other dog." The regiment was known as the "barking dog regiment" because the men had at least three canine mascots. Their names were Colonel, Teaser, and Harvey. All three dogs in this regiment were veteran soldier dogs, but the bull terrier, Harvey, had spent more time in the army than most of his enlisted companions.

The unit adopted Harvey in late 1862. He came to the regiment with First Sergeant Daniel M. Stearns, who earlier had served nearly fourteen months in the Eighth Pennsylvania Reserves. The Terrier's brass dog tag hung from his collar and was inscribed with the words, "I am Lieutenant D.M. Stearns dog. Whose dog are you?" Harvey had accompanied his master's Pennsylvania outfit to the Virginia Peninsula where he was wounded.

On Valentines Day, 1864, Captain William Jordan wrote a letter to his children that told of the pets of the regiment. He told his children that Harvey and Colonel were "veteran soldier dogs" who "go in any of the tents that they want and lay down at night or stand with the sentinels on guard." At the time of the captain's letter Teaser was a new dog.

Other regimental pets included a cat, two tamed raccoons and another squirrel who was kept secured by a tiny chain. Lieutenant Colonel Oscar Sterl owned a pet squirrel who had the run of the camp and would "nibble at the ears" of Harvey and Colonel. One day Teaser attacked this pet squirrel. Harvey picked up the squirrel in his mouth and carried it to safety but the squirrel died of fright shortly after.

On the battlefield, Harvey apparently had an ear for music. The men said that the dog swayed and sang along with their campfire songs. In a letter to his brother in Ohio dated November 18,1864, Private Adam Weaver of Company I wrote that "Old Harvey" had paid him a visit while on picket duty. He also wrote that during the soldiers' campfire sing-alongs, Harvey would bark and move side to side. "My idea is that the noise hurts his ears as it does mine!"

Harvey posing with the 104th's coronet band in Tennessee.

A suttler remembered Harvey and the 104th. He said "They baked bread on a broken piece of flat iron from a rubbish heap and cooked beef by dangling it over fire on sticks or ramrods, so for sure I emptied my supply wagon in no time. I soon took a liking to Harvey, one of three dog mascots…. Harvey'd survived three major skirmishes so far--I near could feel the luck like electricity on his old black tail. I fed Colonel, Teaser, and him handfuls of cush when the men weren't looking--had a good dog myself once, but he got caught in the thresher."

Marcus S. McLemore, a descendant of a member of the 104th Ohio, says Harvey was wounded at least twice. In the summer of 1964 he was wounded and captured near Kennesaw Mountain and returned the next day under a flag of truce. In November of 1864, less than two weeks after Private Weaver wrote about the dog to his brother, Harvey was wounded again in the Battle of Franklin, Tennessee. Luckily he survived and recovered nicely from his wounds.

While serving as an aide to Brigadier General James Reilly, Harvey's owner Lieutenant Stearns was severely injured when his horse fell while jumping the Confederate entrenchments. In January 1865, the 104th was transferred to North Carolina. During this trip Harvey and the regiment lost a companion, when "the blue pup tumbled off the train near Cincinnati." It was probably either Teaser or Colonel who was "the blue pup" referred to in Private Nelson A. Penney's 1886 regimental history.

After the war, the men of the 104th had Harvey's portrait painted for display at reunions and Harvey's image was also incorporated into keepsake buttons. When members of the 104th posed for a group photograph at their 1886 reunion they placed Harvey's picture in the front row. Lieutenant Stearns finished the war as a captain of Company F. He was granted a pension for his Nashville injury and eventually became insane and was committed into the Northern Ohio Insane Asylum, where he died in 1890. Artifacts of the 104th Ohio Volunteer Infantry, including the collar worn by Harvey, are on display in the Massillon Museum in Massillon, Ohio.

5
Stonewall
1st Co. Richmond Howitzer Battalion

Richmond Howitzer Battalion

During the summer of 1862, there was some pretty fierce fighting near and around Richmond, Virginia. During a lull in one such battle, Sergeant Van, a Confederate artillerist, peered through the smoke and saw something waddling out of the woods, making its way to the line of cannoneers of the Richmond Howitzer Battalion. At first he thought it was a baby raccoon or a squirrel. As the creature got closer he saw the white fluff and black spots. It was a puppy.

The puppy ran straight to Sergeant John Van Lew McCreery, who named the puppy Stonewall Jackson. Little Stonewall, like other regiment pets, became very attached to his soldier. Van taught Stonewall to carry around a little pipe clenched in his teeth. He taught the pup that when he removed the pipe from his mouth and inserted it between the toes of his paw it was time to stand at attention for roll call. Stonewall Jackson stood straight and tall, eyes facing forward, until the company was dismissed.

Stonewall, like his namesake, was very intelligent and very brave. When there was a lull in battle he would run about wildly barking at the enemy. The men in the regiment worried about the puppy's safety, so whenever he began to get too close to the firing someone would put him into an ammunition box for safe keeping until the end of the battle.

Richmond Howitzer Battalion

Stonewall's reputation spread throughout the Army of Northern Virginia. The little dog became a victim of elaborate pranks. Other regiments would kidnap him during battle and hide him for the Howitzers to find later. Stonewall was much loved by the men of both the Richmond Howitzer Battalion and the Louisianans of Brigadier Gen. Harry Hays. When the Louisiana troops were sent to a different theatre of war, Stonewall was never seen again. It is not known for sure whether the Louisianans hid him so well he was never found, or more likely they "invited" Stonewall to accompany them.

6
Sallie, 11th PA Volunteer Infantry

Sallie, the mascot of the 11th Pennsylvania Volunteer Infantry, joined the regiment early in the war when she was only four-weeks old. She was a gift to 1st Lt William R. Terry. The regiment was new and training in West Chester. For many of the soldiers it was the first time they were away from their homes and families so they were quick to latch onto the pug-nosed Bull Terrier. Sallie, named after a beautiful girl who lived near the camp, grew up among the men of the regiment. She was an affectionate friend to the men in the unit but did not like civilians or soldiers she did not know. During her time with the 11th PA, Sallie had four litters of puppies, which the men sent to their families back home.

The only known photo of Sallie

The little four-legged soldier knew the drum-roll announcing reveille, and was first out of quarters to attend roll-call. In drills, she latched herself to a particular soldier and pranced alongside him throughout the exercise. At dress-parade, the dog took a position beside the regimental colors. During encampments, she slept by the captain's tent after strolling leisurely through the area on her own kind of inspection. Sallie followed the men on marches and to the battlefield. When her soldiers were in action against the Confederates,

Sallie stood along the front lines barking at the Southerners. Her first battle came in 1862 at Cedar Mountain.

Sallie remained with the colors throughout the engagement. She did the same at Antietam, Fredericksburg, and Chancellorsville. The faithful terrier stood by her men at the Battle of Gettysburg. During the fighting on the first day she became separated from the regiment. The unit suffered heavy losses and was driven back a mile from its original position. In the smoke and confusion the little dog lost her way. Refusing to cross enemy lines, the brave dog returned to the Union battle line at Oak Ridge, where she stood watch over the dead and injured. She remained with her fallen comrades, licking the wounded and guarding the dead until Union forces retook the field from the Confederates. She was found several days later.

Sallie was wounded once during the battle of Spotsylvania Courthouse in May 1864. It was a neck wound and the men called it her "red badge of courage." She continued her faithful service through February 1865. In the Petersburg lines throughout the night of February 5, 1865, Sallie's mournful cries awakened many in the regiment. The next day, during the battle of Hatcher's Run, Virginia, she was killed by a bullet to her head. The weeping men were still under heave fire as they buried their little friend on the battlefield with military honors.

During these years the precocious dog brightened the lives of the soldiers of the regiment. Her service and devotion was not forgotten. Sallie is memorialized by a life-size sculpture lying at the base of the 11th Pennsylvania monument (below and right) erected at Gettysburg in 1890.

7
Grace, 1st (2nd) Maryland CSA

The 1st Maryland CSA suffered nearly 50% casualties during the three day battle at Gettysburg, at some points fighting against friends and relatives in the Federal 1st Maryland Eastern Shore Regiment. Colonel James Wallace of the Union Maryland unit described the event like this: "The 1st Maryland Confederate Regiment met us and were cut to pieces. We sorrowfully gathered up many of our old friends and acquaintances and had them carefully and tenderly cared for."

Included among the honored Confederate dead was Grace, who was listed as "Dog Grace" on roster of the 1st Maryland Artillery. She was the Unit Mascot, a mongrel dog who went into action with the 1st Maryland on July 3rd There were many scattered Rebel dead and wounded after the battle and little Grace was one of them. She was found limping on three legs wandering among the injured soldiers as though looking for her master or perhaps seeking a reason for the horror she had just witnessed. She later died on the field at Culp's Hill. Union Brigadier General Thomas Kane (left) wrote of the scene:

"She licked someone's hand after being perfectly riddled with bullets. Regarding her as the only Christian-minded being on either side, I ordered her to be honorably buried."

General Kane included the incident of the dog charging with the Confederates in his official report.

"The canine that accompanied the 1st Maryland was regrettably killed in action on July 3 at Culp's Hill, after having participated in the charge of the regiment. So struck by the animal's gallantry and loyalty to its human companions, a Union officer ordered the animal be given a proper burial alongside the dead of 1st Maryland."

The report was enclosed in a letter dated March 28, 1874, sent to Peter Frederick Rothermel by Kane's wife, Elizabeth D. Kane. The painting on page 24 below represents Rothermel's interpretation of the fighting on Culp's Hill on the morning of July 3rd. Rothermel used accounts provided by Union eye witnesses to this charge to create the painting and the dog's presence in the charge was also noted by several former officers and men who replied to him.

Towards the right center, he included Grace just in front of the Confederate lines. The painting is currently on display at Pennsylvania State Museum in Harrisburg.

Repulse of General Johnson's Division by General Geary's White Star Division, by Peter Frederick Rothermel, 1870

On the northeastern slope of Culp's Hill at Gettysburg rests a marker that reads 2nd Maryland CSA however it was not the 2nd Maryland who fought there, it was the First Maryland Confederate Battalion. About 20 years after the war, the Confederate 1st Maryland wanted to erect a monument to honor their comrades. They met resistance from Union foes because there was already a monument to the Federal 1st Maryland. Since both units fought on Culp's Hill the Union unit was afraid here would be some confusion if there were two monuments. The Confederates agreed to rename their unit "2nd" Maryland." Most people just glance at the monument, but if you take a very close look you will see that the Confederates carved the words *"1st MD changed to"* just above the words 2nd Maryland.

8
Salem, 13th Illinois Infantry
"Fremont's Grey Hounds"

Captain Henry T. Noble (left) took Ned, his Newfoundland dog, into the army with him. The dog was in his glory while on the march and was delighted to skirmish through the woods by the roadside and scatter the masked batteries of "Secesh", but sometimes he had to fall back on his reserves for support. Eventually Captain Noble sent Ned home because he was afraid he would be lost. There was a second dog with the Thirteenth Illinois, a little black one, who chased spent cannon shot at Wilson's Creek, He used his paws to try to stop the balls. But the third dog, Salem, was the real dog of the regiment.

After a very long and tedious march the Thirteenth turned to the south and camped for one day, May 1st 1862 in the town of Salem, Arkansas. On the morning of May 2d, the men were ready to march but did not start until 1:00 pm. When they started the march a mischievous little Irishman, Peter Dougdale of Company H, took away something from the town concealed in his shirt. It was a small puppy. Salem got his name from the town where he was born. Whether Peter Dougdale's love for pets caused him to tote away this small canine or whether it was a spur of the moment idea we will never know, but we do know that the other boys were happy Peter took him and they all volunteered to help take care of the little puppy through the dog days that were coming on and they declared that "EVERY DOG MUST HAVE HIS DAY"

After a day or two the puppy was assigned quarters in the feed box of the wagons and from that time onward he was known as the dog of the regiment. His amusing antics as a puppy endeared him to his friends and his development towards doghood was watched with great interest. One of the men described Salem like this: *"He was shaggy about the head and shoulders But his color, aye, there's the rub, he was not a yaller dog, neither was he a red dog, one need not be offended if he was called a reddish brown, but he certainly did not have a terra cotta color. In fact one would not be far out of the way to say that his color was something like the worst painted house in town."*

Some men of the 13th Illinois Infantry

Salem grew to be a middle-sized dog with a body built for quick action and great endurance. He had eyes that smiled at his friends but flashed fire and sparks at those who provoked him. He soon began to develop an unusual shrewdness. Salem knew unerringly every person who belonged to the camp and that it was only necessary to say "Salem, there is a stranger in camp" and he would set out and search until he found him and drove him out of camp. His careful training in camp gave him a loyalty that could not be shaken. When in battle the zip of bullets excited him and he would savagely snap at them as they whizzed near him. Historians have not been able to determine Salem's fate but it is probable that Salem failed to board the boat with the men during one of the regiment's many steamboat expeditions.

9
Traveler and Jefferson Davis

Jefferson Davis loved all kinds of animals and birds. The grounds were full of his pet peacocks and he saved all the leftover bits of food from his table to feed them. His dressing gown pockets were always overflowing with grain for his feathered friends. Every morning Mr. Davis walked along a short pavement leading from the back door of his home. He told his friends "It is just the length of my exercise path in prison." His flock of peacocks followed him up and down the path. One old cock would open his beautiful tail and follow close behind as if to court him. In 1855, President Franklin Pierce gave a Japanese spaniel to his Secretary of War Jefferson Davis, who would later become the president of the Confederacy. Many years later, Mrs. Davis recalled that as puppies such dogs were so small "that a coffee saucer made an ample scampering ground for them." Mr. Davis was very fond of his pets, but his true love was his dog, Traveler.

A very interesting story followed Traveler to Jefferson Davis' house. Samuel W. Dorsey was the man from whom Mr. Davis purchased his home, which was called Beauvoir. Mr. Dorsey had a wife named Sarah (left) and the couple traveled all over the world. They purchased Traveler, whose father was a Russian Bulldog, as a young puppy while visiting the Alps. The pup was trained to be Mrs. Dorsey's bodyguard and went everywhere with them.

One time the Dorseys were on a camping trip in the Arabian Desert. Mr. Dorsey realized that one of his Arabian servants was stealing from him and had the man severely punished. The next day, Mr. Dorsey and some of the Arabians went on a two days' journey, leaving Mrs. Dorsey and the camp in the charge of an old Arab sheik. That night, while asleep under the tent, Traveler began barking fiercely and Mrs. Dorsey woke up. She then heard a man scream. She sprang from her cot, quickly got a light, and found a man pinned down to the ground by Traveler. It was the Arab who had been beaten by Mr. Dorsey's orders. There was a huge knife lying beside him. He had cut his way into the tent and crept in to wreak his vengeance upon her for the beating he received.

Another incident like this occurred while Mrs. Dorsey was in Paris. She attended a reception at the Tulleries wearing magnificent diamond jewelry. On her return to the hotel she went at once to her room. While her husband and some friends were outside smokeing, Mrs. Dorsey quickly fell asleep. She was once again awakened by a sound of a desperate struggle on the floor, where Traveler had succeeded in pinning down a thief who had followed her, attracted by the glitter of her diamonds. This man was one of the worst characters in Paris. Before he could be hung, he died of the wound in his throat torn by Traveler's teeth.

After Mr. Dorsey died, Traveler was given to Jefferson Davis (right) and became his constant companion and guard. He allowed no one to come onto the pproperty whose good intent he had any reason to suspect. The entire place was under his care; not a window or door needed to be locked or barred because everything was safe while Traveler was on guard. He patrolled wide porches that surrounded the house on every side.

If Mr. Davis wished to safeguard a friend staying at his home and give him the freedom of the place, day or night, he would put one hand on the person's shoulder and the other on the dog's head and say: "Traveler, this is my friend." The dog would accept the introduction very gravely, would smell his clothes and hands and "size him up." He never forgot, and from then on Mr. Davis' "friend" was safe to come and go as he pleased.

As fierce as the dog was, and as bloody as was his record, he was as gentle as a lamb with little children. Mrs. Davis' small niece, a child about two years old, made the dog her playmate, and the baby and the dog would merrily roll together on the grass. She would pull his hair, pound on his head, or ride around the place on his back, the dog trotting as coolly as a Shetland pony. This child lived some distance down the beach; but she went home day after day in perfect safety, guarded and guided by Traveler.

Traveler liked to rush around chasing fiddler crabs, which was a funny hobby of his, and would bark and throw up the sand with his paws in triumph when he had succeeded in driving a bunch of crabs into the sea. But even fiddler crabs had no attraction for Traveler when he went to walk with Mr. Davis. He was then a bodyguard, pure and simple, and had all the dignity and watchfulness of a squad of soldiers detailed as escorts. When Mr. Davis would become buried in thought, oblivious to surroundings, Traveler had to be on high alert. If Mr. Davis would walk very close to the water, Traveler would gently take his trousers leg in his teeth or would jump between him and the sea to call attention to the big waves coming in.

One day Traveler seemed very droopy and in pain. Mr. Davis could not make the dog comfortable so he wrote a note to a friend who was the most celebrated physician in that part of the country. The doctor came, but nothing seemed to relieve the dog's suffering. All night he moaned and cried, looking up into Mr. Davis's face with big, pathetic eyes, as if begging for help from the hand that had never before failed him. All those long hours, Mrs. Dorsey, Mr. Davis, and the doctor kept their hopeless watch. Just at daylight he died, his head on Mr. Davis' knee and his master's tears falling like rain upon the faithful beast. As Mr. Davis gently laid the dead dog upon the rug, he said softly: "I have indeed lost a friend." Traveler was put in a coffin-like box, and the whole family was present at the funeral. Mr. Davis sorrowfully patted the box with his hand, and then turned away before it was lowered into the ground. The dog was buried in the front yard of Beauvoir. A small stone, beautifully engraved, marked the place. At some time during the intervening years, that stone has unfortunately disappeared.

10
Fido and Abraham Lincoln

Abraham Lincoln was often seen around the town with his dog Fido. When Mr. Lincoln went to the market, trailing behind carrying a parcel in his mouth was Fido. Mr. Lincoln would sometimes stop for a haircut, and Fido would wait outside the barbershop with the other customers' pets. Fido was the type of dog who loved attention and would spend countless minutes chasing his own tail.

Fido was a floppy-eared, rough-coated, yellowish dog. He was about 7 years old when Lincoln was elected president of the United States on November 6, 1860. Although Fido was a friendly dog, he was fearful of many things, like church bells, gunshots and even trains sounds, and the loud cannons, which had announced his presidential nomination, had terrified Fido, so when the Lincoln family was ready to move to Washington DC, Mr. Lincoln was worried about taking Fido on such a long train ride. Mr. Lincoln's son, Tad, tried in vain  to convince his father to take the dog to Washington. Finally, the president-elect decided to give Fido to two neighbor boys, John and Frank Roll. The Lincolns knew them well. The two families were good friends and the boys' father, John Eddy Roll, was a carpenter who had helped the Lincolns remodel their house

Although Lincoln trusted the boys to take good care of Fido he did set down some rules. They were asked never to scold Fido for entering the house with muddy paws. He was not to be tied up alone in the backyard. Fido was to be allowed into the Roll home whenever he scratched at the front door, and he was to be allowed into the Rolls' dining room at mealtimes. Fido was used to being given food by everyone sitting around the table. To make Fido feel at home, the Lincolns gave the Rolls their horsehair sofa. Shortly before the Lincolns left for the White House, they took Fido to F.W. Ingmire's studio in Springfield to have his picture taken. Mr. Ingmire draped a piece of fancy material over a washstand and placed Fido on top. Willie and Tad watched the proceedings but did not get into the pictures.

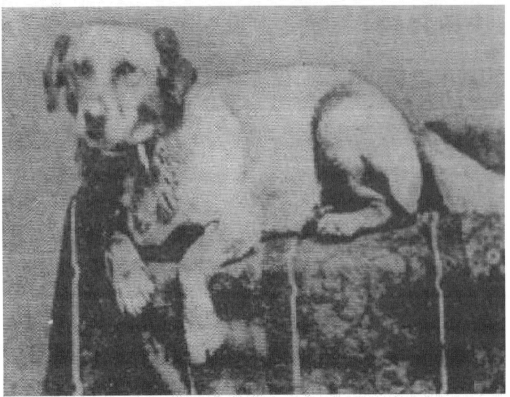

Reassuring news regarding Fido came from Illinois late in 1863. On December 27, 1863, the president's Springfield barber, William Florville, wrote the Lincolns a letter saying, "Tell Taddy that his dog is alive and kicking doing well. He stays mostly at John E. Rolls with his boys who are about the size now that Tad & Willy were when they left for Washington."
After the tragic assassination in 1865, hundreds of out-of-town visitors, in Springfield for the funeral, crowded around the Lincoln home. On this tragic occasion, John Roll brought Fido back to his original home to meet the mourners that were there. Fido passed away less than a year after Mr. Lincoln was assassinated.

11
Sergeant William H. Brown's Dog

John Covode (left) was born on March 18, 1808, near West Fairfield, Westmoreland County, Pennsylvania He was the abolitionist member of Congress who was first elected to the US House of Representatives as a Whig in 1855, was re-elected as a Republican in 1857, and again in 1857, 1859, 1861 and 1867. On February 9, 1870, the U. S. House of Representatives declared him duly elected, whereupon he qualified, serving until his death on January 11, 1871.

Sergeant William H. Brown was born in Philadelphia, Pennsylvania. In 1860, he was living in the 2nd ward of Philadelphia. He was a wheelwright, and he had $200 in personal property. He was living with his wife Susan and their children, Mary, William H, Emma and Clara. He was 5 feet 5-1/2 inches tall, and had a fair complexion, blue eyes, and brown hair. He had a scar on his breast from a blister. When he was 25 years old he enlisted. Sergeant Brown was wounded on December 13, 1862, at Fredericksburg, Virginia. He died near Fredericksburg, of those wounds, on that same day. The next Monday, December 15, a dog was found near his body. The following article appeared in the Saturday Evening Post on December 27, 1862. A slightly different version was published in the Philadelphia Inquirer on December 19, 1862.

Singular Fidelity of a Dog on the Battle-Field.

On Monday last, as Hon. John Covode, in company with a number of officers, was passing over the battle-field beyond Fredericksburg, their attention was called to a small dog lying by a corpse. Mr. Covode halted a few minutes to see if life was extinct. Raising the coat from the man's face, he found him dead.

The dog, looking wistfully up, ran to the dead man's face and kissed his silent lips. Such devotion in a small dog was so singular that Mr. Covode examined some papers upon the body, and found it to be that of Sergeant W. H. Brown, Company C, Pennsylvania, 91st Regiment.

The dog was shivering with the cold, but refused to leave his master's body, and as the coat was thrown over his face again he seemed very uneasy, and tried to get under it to the man's face. He had, it seems, followed the regiment into battle, and stuck to his master, and when he fell remained with him, refusing to leave him or to eat anything.

As the party returned an ambulance was carrying the corpse to a little grove of trees for interment, and the little dog following, the only mourner at that funeral, as the hero's comrades had been called to some other point.

12
Curly, 11th Ohio Infantry

Curly was a water spaniel (right), chocolate brown with a few white spots, big, beautiful brown eyes, wide, intelligent forehead, with a white face. On April 19th, 1861, Mrs. John Shellabarger gave him to John Crouse of Company A of the 11th Ohio Infantry. She said she had far too many dogs, so Curly had to go. John Crouse brought him to camp after Mrs. Shellabarger said Curly was "no good on earth for anything I know of; so he ought to make a good soldier." All the men in his regiment quickly fell in love with him. Curly was included in the company roster and went  with them to West Virginia, where he took an active part in the campaigns of the regiment. He was always in the advance, and during a skirmish would run between the lines barking, as if to let everyone know that the rebels over there were no friends of his.

On August 17, 1862, the regiment left camp Piatt on steamers and headed down the Kanahawa toward the Ohio. Heading up that stream the men soon jumped to the conclusion that Gen. J.D. Cox was taking them east. By this time each company owned one or more dogs, and they were getting to be a burden. The officer in charge thought it was about time to unload the mongrel brood. He had a man detailed that night to throw every dog overboard and let him swim for his life. The detail reported to the major "If I throw Company A's dog overboard I will be a goner for sure." So that much of the order was revoked and Curly was saved. When the boats got as far as Blennerhasset's Island, the regiment had to disembark and Curly marched to Parkersburg, West Virginia with them. From there they rode a B. & O. stock car to Harper's Ferry. Curly stuck to his command at second Bull Run, Frederick City, Sand Mountain and Antietam, then back to Clarksburg, West Virginia.

Some men of the Ohio Infantry

A few men were target practicing one afternoon when Curly ran into the bushes behind the target. Captain Staley fired and caught Curly in the neck. Captain Hatfield detailed a nurse and Curly was placed in a wagon, carefully nursed, and soon reported for duty. At Chickamauga, Curly stayed on the field to take care of the wounded. He did this for the men ever since he was wounded himself because he knew how it felt to be hurt. As Curly passed from one wounded sufferer to another he ignored the confederates who tempted him with bits of food to leave his comrades. When General Thomas arranged for the parole and return of those who were wounded, Curly took advantage of the flag of truce, and came in with the unfortunates.

Here is where Curly ran into some trouble. A captain of another regiment, the Tenth Ohio, saw Curly and wanted him for his own pet. The captain tied Curly up to his tent. When the boys of company A heard the dog came in with the wounded they went to look for him. They found him tied up to the tent, but the captain claimed the dog as his and refused let him go. The colonel of the Tenth heard the men and went over to see what the ruckus was all about. Jule Ogier spoke for Curly and asked that he be given back to Company A, which the colonel ordered done, and the dog rushed to his friends and took his place at the campfire and mess table where he belonged.

.

In 1864, as the regiment was on their way home from Mission Ridge, Curly fell out of a car while in motion somewhere near Bowling Green, Kentucky. A few men went back for him and found poor Curly with a leg broken. He was carefully patched up and returned to Dayton, where he found a home with his old comrade, Baggot. The men of the 11th wanted Curly at all reunions, so Baggot took him. Later he was sent to the central branch of the National Soldiers Home in Dayton. He was happy there and lived to the ripe old age of twelve years. He died among his soldier friends and they buried him on the beautiful grounds of the Soldiers Home.

13
Brigadier General Alexander Asboth
and York

Federal General Alexander S. Asboth was a brave and chivalrous gentleman of a kind and noble disposition. He met everyone, even the regular volunteers in the army, with extreme courtesy. Historian William Watson Davis said of Asboth: "When not engaged in the barbarous practice of pillaging, Asboth was a refined yet amusing fellow with a great love for flowers and a keen interest in dogs and fine horses." He was known throughout the army by his huge iron-gray mustache and side-whiskers, and by the blanket of camel's hair, with large and slightly faded black and white stripes, which he always wore in place of an overcoat. His faithful friend, York, a large Saint Bernard, usually accompanied him wherever he went. Eyewitnesses have said that Asboth, while stationed in Pensacola, always fed his dog from the table. A lover of animals, he also sent unique animals from his various posts back to New York to expand the collection of the Central Park Zoo. The zoo's first Florida black bear, for example, was captured by Asboth somewhere in Northwest Florida and sent to New York by ship.

In late 1861 and early 1862, Fayetteville, Arkansas first began experiencing the real impact of occupying armies. Confederate troops made winter camp to the south at Boston Mountain. The Union remained to the north near the Missouri border. After the Rebels began a push toward the opposing force, they issued what amounted to a retreat through Fayetteville. Along the way they set fire to the city in an attempt to keep the Union from finding anything of use there. Following that incident came the first appearance of Union soldiers in Fayetteville. It was a scouting division led by General Asboth who visited Jonas Tebbetts' house. Jonas' daughter, Miriam, was upset about the soldiers in her home and in her diary wrote about Asboth's visit. What bothered her most was that the General and his dog, York, ate the family's last jar of strawberry preserves.

York fought with his master throughout the battle of Pea Ridge, Arkansas, March 6th-8th, 1862. He ran beside the general's horse, refusing to leave his side. One eyewitness was so impressed that he sketched the scene shown below. The drawing was later published in *Leslie's Illustrated Newspaper*. The other officers in the sketch are Acting Brigadier General Albert, Brigade Quartermaster McKay and Major George E. Waring, Jr.

In the battle of Marianna on September 27, 1864, Asboth received debilitating wounds to his arm and face. He wrote in his official report to Major George B. Drake: "I myself was also honored by the rebels with two balls, the first, in the face, breaking the cheek bone, the other fracturing my left arm in two places." Due to the scope of his injuries, he had to withdraw from field duty. The serious nature of the wounds did not keep him from the war. Asboth recovered sufficiently to resume command. Towards the end of the war, he was brevetted major-general

14
Louis Pfieff's Dog

Some regimental dogs were picked up along the way but many were pets brought from the soldiers' homes. One of the soldiers who brought his dog along when he enlisted was Louis Pfieff. The men of the Illinois regiment soon adopted the Pfieff pup as their mascot. The men even included the dog in the photo they had taken with their new Henry Rifles.

On April 6th, 1862, Confederate forces led by General Johnston attacked General Grant's army at Pittsburgh Landing, better known as Shiloh. The Union forces, including Louis Pfieff's regiment and their loyal mascot, were surprised and not prepared to fight but they still managed to hold their own until reinforcements arrived. The Confederates lost their leader when a stray bullet killed General Johnston. On the second day, April 7th, Grant launched a counterattack and the Confederates retreated to Corinth. It was a victory for the Union forces. Approximately 23,746 men died in the Battle of Shiloh. Of those, 13,047 were Union soldiers. Among the dead was Louis Pfieff.

Travel was hard in 1862, especially for a lady traveling alone, but Mrs. Louis Pfieff, like many women who became widows after the Battle of Shiloh, traveled all the way from Chicago to Tennessee to find her dear husband's dead body. Mrs. Pfieff was determined that her husband's remains should be returned to his home for reburial. When she arrived at the battlefield, she searched tirelessly among the markers of the thousands of hastily dug graves of the Union troops that had died during the two days of fierce fighting on April 6 and 7. After many long and sorrowful hours of searching she was unable to find her husband's body. She asked many people, both soldiers and civilians, if they knew him or had seen his name on a marker but no one was able to help her. Discouraged and grief stricken, Mrs. Pfieff looked across the burial ground toward the horizon and through tearful eyes she noticed something coming toward her. At first she thought it was her imagination, but then realized it was a large dog. As it came closer she was surprised to see that it was her own dog, the one that her husband had taken with him when he left Illinois. The dog was happy to see her and she knelt and hugged it, crying and burying her face in its fur.

Suddenly the dog jumped away from her, looking back at her and barking as if to say "follow me." Mrs. Pfieff followed her dog all the way to the far end of the field to an unmarked grave by a Poplar tree; it's yellow flowers just starting to bloom. Mrs. Pfieff requested that the grave be opened and sure enough, the grave contained the remains of Lt. Pfieff. She later learned that the dog had been by her husband's side when he was killed, and had been keeping vigil at his burial site for 12 days, leaving his post only long enough to find food and drink.

15
Mike, The Blackmith's Dog

Patrick Colligan was born in Ireland about 1840. He immigrated to the United States in 1855. By 1860, he was employed as a blacksmith in Rutland, VT where he lived with Daniel Conway, a blacksmith, and his family. On 2 May 1861 Patrick mustered in for three months as a private in Company G, First Regiment of the Vermont Infantry. After his three months of duty were completed, he was mustered out of the military on 15 Aug 1861, but voluntarily re-enlisted. By November, he was in Burlington, VT where he was mustered into Captain Perkins' Company, First Regiment of Vermont Calvary. This time he held the rank of blacksmith, and maintained this rank throughout the rest of his military service.

During the war, Patrick had a pet dog named Mike. Mike deemed himself a scout and made trips ahead of the cavalry to look for the enemy. He loved the booming of the cannons and crack of the muskets. Mike was sitting on the seat of a Union ammunition wagon when the "Rebs" shot the horses. Mike sustained a shattered front leg, but survived. He lost the tip of his tail at the battle of Kelly's Ford. He made many other trips between the two lines of soldiers and survived the war and returned home with a hero's welcome.

During the war, 22-year-old Edwin Forbes was a staff artist for Frank Leslie's Illustrated Newspaper. For two years he followed the Army of the Potomac sketching whatever he thought would be of interest to the people reading the newspaper. When Edwin wanted to sketch a Calvary blacksmith shop he came upon Patrick. As he was drawing he became intrigued with a bossy little dog who seemed to be supervising the blacksmiths. Forbes and added Mike to his sketch right in the center of the scene.

16
Captain Werner Von Bachelle's Dog

During the Civil War, a number of ethnically oriented militia groups responded to President Lincoln's call for volunteers to preserve the union. One such unit was a predominantly German unit known as the Citizens Corps of Milwaukee. On April 25, 1861, William Lindwurm, Frederick Schumacher and Werner Von Bachelle were commissioned the unit officers. By May 10 1861, the company was officially mustered into the 6th Wisconsin Regiment as Company F, bringing the total of German-Americans in the Union Army to almost thirty-six thousand. The brigade, in 1862, achieved increased efficiency and military prowess and a distinctive uniform that resulted in the nickname "Black Hat Brigade" from other Union soldiers. Following the brigade's determined assault at South Mountain, the brigade won a new title, "The Iron Brigade of the West". Three days later, the unit proved its worth once again by bravely assaulting Lee's forces in one of the bloodiest battles of the war.

Everyone in his unit knew how much Von Bachelle, an ex-officer of the French army, loved animals. So when a Newfoundland dog wandered into camp one day; of course, it was given to officer Von Bachelle. Von Bachelle loved the dog and trained him to perform military salutes and many other remarkable things. In camp, on the march and in the line of battle, this dog was his constant companion. The two became inseparable and were together on the morning of September 17, 1862, during battle at Antietam. The morning was the bloodiest of the three phases of the battle. While at the farthest point of his companies advance, near the Miller Farm along the Hagerstown Pike, Captain Von Bachelle led his men into a cornfield. He was shot several times and would die on the spot. As the men fell back they called for the dog. The animal would not leave Von Bachelle's side in spite of the heavy fire from rifle and cannon. Two days later their bodies were recovered, the dog's body lying across his master's.

Rufus Dawes, then major of the regiment wrote, "At the very farthest point of advance on the turnpike, Captain Werner Von Bachelle, commanding company F, was shot dead. His soldierly qualities commanded the respect of all, and his loss was deeply felt in the regiment. The dog was by his side when he fell. Our line of men left the body when they retreated, but the dog stayed with his dead master, and was found upon the morning of the 19th of September lying dead upon his body. We buried him with his master. So far as we know, no family or friends mourned poor Bachelle, and it is probable that he was joined in death by his most devoted friend on earth." Von Bachelle is buried in the officer's section of Antietam National Cemetery. It is believed his dog is buried with him.

17
Hero of Castle Thunder

Castle Thunder, located in Richmond, Virginia was a prison used by the Confederacy to house civilian prisoners, including captured Union spies, political prisoners and those charged with treason. The building was a converted tobacco warehouse located on Tobacco Row. A large number of its inmates were sentenced to death. Even though the inmates were sometimes allowed boxes of medicine and other supplies, the prison guards had a reputation for brutality.

A Union Soldier in the prison wrote this poem about it:

On Cary Street, in Richmond, there is a mongrel den
Of thieves, sneaks and cowards mixed up with gentlemen.
Oh what a living shame to huddle in together
Men and beasts, wild and tame, like birds of every feather!
The Reb authorities scared up this greatest wonder,
Made it a prison, and named it Castle Thunder.

Captain George W. Alexander was in charge. An eccentric character, Capt. Alexander was not especially well liked. Reputed to be a corrupt and cruel disciplinarian, Alexander was said to have a heart as dark as the clothing he wore. He was fond of dramatic apparel, wearing tight black trousers buckled at the knee, black stockings and a flowing black shirt. He rode a black horse and kept a large black dog, a hound called Hero by some and Nero by others. The dog was so intimidating to prisoners that he was rumored to be meaner than a bear in a fight.

All of the prisoners realized that an escape from the Castle meant certain recapture within a few hours. Writings in the letters and diaries of over fifty soldiers state that a monster bloodhound was kept at Castle Thunder to pursue Union prisoners who might try to escape. Jet-black, standing over three feet in height, with a huge but well-proportioned head and body, Hero presented a very formidable appearance, and was doubtless an efficient guard to the rebel prison. His weight is said to be about 180 pounds. He was as well known as any of the crabbed officials themselves, and was respected accordingly.

The May 19, 1865 issue of the Richmond *Whig* described the beast like this:

"Hero is a dog about seven feet in length from tip to top, weighing nearly two hundred pounds. He is a splendid cross between a Russian bloodhound and a bull-dog, and combines the faithfulness of the one with the ferocity of the other. We have seen him seize little dogs that came around his heels, shake them and cast them twenty feet from him. The stoutest man he would bring to the ground by one grip on the throat, and it was always a difficult matter to get him off if he had once tasted or smelled blood."

Now for the true story of this killer beast. Version 1:The dog was brought to Richmond the year before the war on a Russian ship. He was an animal of immense size and was used in Polish Russia to hunt wild boars. He was considered a great curiosity in Richmond and had five different owners before he reached the commandant of Castle Thunder. His dogship belonged originally to Joseph Mayo, late Mayor, and by him was loaned to Capt. G. W. Alexander, at one time Commandant of the Castle post. He was the soul of good nature and would play with anyone who would notice him. Reverend J. L. Burrows was a chaplain at Castle Thunder. He said he had petted the dog many times. The reverend stated he was *"one of the best natured hounds whose head I had ever petted.... And one of the most cowardly... if a small terrier barked a him he would put his tale between his legs... he was quite playful with the prisoners when permitted to walk around them."* All four of Hero's owners before Mayo stated he was never known to bite a person. He was a sweet old hound who loves adults and children alike. Hero had a theatrical side to him. He performed a dog's part in the play of the "Virginia Cavalier," at the New Theatre. Abandoning the stage, Hero returned to his post as sentinel at the Castle, and remained up to the evening of Monday, April 3, 1865. As for the dog chasing prisoners it never happened. (It was only at rare intervals that a Union prisoner escaped and these were speedily intercepted by Confederate pickets on patrol.) When the war closed an old gentleman named Mr. Chilvers who lived in Henrico County, seven miles out of Richmond, owned the dog. A Sidney Munn, who had heard of the dog went out to buy him but when Mr. Chilvers would not sell him, the soldier took both Mr. Chilvers and Hero north to New York. He advertised the beast as the terrible bloodhound used to recapture escaped prisoners and no doubt made much money. Mr. Chilvers returned to Richmond at the end of seven months with three thousand dollars in greenbacks as his share of the profits leaving the dog to continue his tour. He was trained to fight a bear and made $12,000 for one bear fight in which he was victorious. A man named Sam Ward had one of his puppies and this was stolen from him, carried North, advertised and shown with the father.

Version 2: Similar to version 1 except that Hero was brought to New York as a prisoner of war when he was captured in Richmond. George D. Putnum was a prisoner at Castle Thunder when he saw the dog taken away by "Weitzel's troops." An article in the York Times in 1865 said that Mr. Munn was a sutler of the 140th New York regiment and captured Hero in Richmond sending him North, a prisoner of war. Mr. Childers is not mentioned here, however all the resources I found place Hero in New York making money with Mr. Munn.

18
Brigadier General Bryan Grimes
and the St. Bernard

At Cold Harbor, Virginia, in June 1864, Confederate Brigadier General Bryan Grimes (left) came across Bernard protecting the corpse of a Pennsylvania colonel. The dog won instant popularity with the 14th North Carolina Infantry and remained with the unit for more than two years. In a letter to his wife, General Grimes wrote:

"…..Gen. Hill, seeing a battery and not being positive whether they were Jackson's men expected at that point or the enemy, ordered a flag forward to be waved. When I took the flag of the 4th regiment and galloped my horse towards the battery, when they opened with the whole battery on the line in column, in my rear, and here was on the extreme left of the long continuous line of battle and kept the enemy in check, until late in the afternoon there came an order to charge! and forward they went. My horse was killed and I continued on foot, driving the enemy from his breastworks through their camps, taking their artillery and supplying myself with another horse.

Here I captured a fine St. Bernard dog, which was protecting the corpse of a Colonel of a Pennsylvania regiment, who upon inspection was found to have on steel breast plates, which had protected him so long as his face was to the fire, but upon retreating had received a mortal wound in the rear...."

General Grimes saved the breastplate *"as a memento of the battlefield and Yankee cowardice."* He named the captured dog "General" and It became the regiment's mascot. General accompanied Grimes through many of he army's most difficult campaigns. Unfortunately in 1864, General "succumbed to the hard marching, broke down and was lost, not having the endurance of men."

After the war, Grimes returned to North Carolina and settled briefly in Raleigh. He subsequently moved back to Grimesland in January 1867 and resumed farming. In the course of the Civil War, General Grimes had six horses shot from under him. His wife, Charlotte, said, "My husband always had a strong affinity for animals. He used to say is horse, Warren, had as much sense as a human being." Warren lived many years after the war and died at age 28. Grimes had him buried in the family burying ground. In 1880, Grimes was ambushed and killed by a hired assassin named William Parker, apparently to keep him from testifying at a criminal trial. Parker was later acquitted, but was lynched by an angry mob. Grimes was buried in the family cemetery on his plantation.

19
Irish Wolfhounds of the Irish Brigade

The 69th New York Militia was formed in 1851. After service at the battle of Bull Run in July of 1861, they were reformed as the 69th New York State Volunteer Infantry. "The 69th" was named the 1st Regiment of the soon to be famous Irish Brigade, and fought with great valor at every major battle of the Army of the Potomac. The Irish Wolfhound is the Irish Brigade's hereditary mascot. Known as the Great Dog of Ireland, Wolfhounds were companions to the Kings of Ireland, and are prominently featured on the original coat of arms and badges of the regiment. These dogs are said to be a match for any wolf on earth. It was the traits and disposition of the Irish Wolfhound that inspired the 69th Regimental Motto "Gentle When Stroked, Fierce When Provoked".

The unit's Regimental crest depicts the 1861 Regimental dress cap device, two Irish Wolfhounds, and the red shamrock of the First Division of the Second Corps of the Army of the Potomac in the Civil War. These separated by a rainbow depicting the units service as a founding regiment of the 42nd Rainbow Division in World War I. The Green background is a unique honor; most infantry units are required to have an infantry blue background. The regiment has this because its Civil War Regimental colors (flags) were green with the Golden Harp of Ireland.

First photograph of a religious service in the U.S. Army:
Mass in the field for the soldiers of the 69th New York Regiment prior
to the first Battle of Bull Run in July 1861.

They participated in the Battle of Bull Run (Manassas), the Peninsula Campaign, Fair Oaks, Mechanicsville, Gaines' Mill, Malvern Hill, Antietam (Sharpsburg), Fredericksburg, Chancellorsville, and Gettysburg, Following Gettysburg, the Irish Brigade ceased to exist as a functioning unit and was disbanded in June 1864. The depleted ranks of the 69th Regiment were filled with new volunteers, as well as draftees from New York's Irish ghettoes. At the end of the summer of 1864, the 69th rejoined its Irish comrades as 1st Regiment of the 2nd Irish Brigade. The brigade served until the end of the war and was present at the surrender of General Lee at Appomattox. Out of more than 2,000 regiments that served with the Union Army, the 69th lost more men than all but six regiments.

On March 17, 1953, two Irish Wolfhounds were adopted by the 69th as Regimental Mascots. They are clad in green coats with the gold numerals "69", and parade immediately to the rear of the Regimental Color Guard. After the Civil War the 69th New York continued on, serving in the Mexican-American war and both World Wars. Today, they are known as the 1st Battalion 69th Infantry (Mechanized) New York Army National Guard. General Robert E. Lee christened this unit "The Fighting 69th" for good reason. The 69th is one of the most decorated Units in the United States Army with 63 Battle Rings, 28 Campaign Streamers and 7 Medals of Honor to it's credit. An Irish wolfhound is memorialized on the Irish Brigade monument at Gettysburg.

20
Tip, Major and the Cameron Highlanders

The 79th New York Cameron Highlanders was started in the mid 19th century and consisted primarily of emigrant Scots, Irish, and persons of Celtic heritage. The New Yorkers wore the Cameron of Erracht tartan and adopted the numerical designation of 79 after the British 79th Cameron Highlanders. In May, 1861, just after the Battle of Fort Sumter, they numbered 795 men. By the end of the war the number of men killed, wounded and missing totaled 502. The 79th was well respected as a hard fighting regiment throughout the war. A history of the regiment would not be complete without mentioning Tip and Major. Everyone in the brigade knew Tip. He was born in Beaufort, South Carolina and served out the three years term of the regiment returning with them to New York in 1864. He was named Tip because he a peculiarity in his tail; however one report said he was missing part of a hind leg. Although he was a friend to all the soldiers in the 79th, his special owner was William Samo of the drum corps who loved Tip like a son. Tip was familiar with and friendly to all members of the regiment but he could never be induced to extend his friendship to the Michiganders…. he drew the line at the Highlanders. During campaigns in Virginia, Kentucky, Mississippi, and Tennessee, Tip did an excellent job in the foraging line bringing many pigs, sheep, and chickens to the mess kettles. During dress parade he would accompany the band and drum corps as they marched down the line walking as demurely as the oldest veteran and on the return, when the corps played a quick step, he proved that he was just as well versed in the cadence step as any of the musicians.

Major was another dog attached to the drum corps. His name frequently made people laugh because it reminded them of all the funny things Tip did. One day Major was sunning himself in front of Major Morrison's quarters when Major Morrison and Major Hagadorn stepped from the tent. At that moment some one from a tent called out "Major" when all three quickly turned in the direction of the voice, each thinking for a moment that he was the party addressed. In order to officially seal Major as one of the corps and to establish his identity in case he went astray, the picture of a drum was painted on one of his sides and D.C. 7 9 was painted on the other.

On 2 September, 1863, the Highlanders took the key rail city of Knoxville. To defend the city from Rebel assault, the Union troops built several forts and the 79th and others occupied Fort Sanders, an existing fort,(known by the Confederates as Fort Loudon). The position, a bastioned earthwork, was on top of a hill, which formed a salient at the northeast corner of the town's defenses. In front of the earth- work was a 12-foot-wide ditch, some ten feet deep, with an almost vertical slope to the top of the parapet, about 15 feet above the bottom of the ditch. The fort was defended by 12 guns and, according to different sources, 250 or 440 troops, of which the 79th provided 120 men. Luckily for the Highlanders Tip liked to take walks with his master outside the fort.

The night of November 28th General Longstreet ordered the brigades of Humphrey's Mississippians and Bryan and Wofford's Georgians, approximately 3,000 men, to make a surprise attack on the fort. It was bitterly cold as the Confederate troops quietly moved into position just 150 yards from the fort but, in spite of their caution, the defenders overheard them and were prepared for the coming assault. Learning of the attack early enough, preparations were made in defense of the fort. General Longstreet had spied a Highlander walking the dog, probably Tip and William Samo, directly into the fort. Not knowing that Tip and Private Samo had walked on a plank, Longstreet assumed the fort was not guarded by a ditch. This mistake was to cost the Rebs the battle. Longstreet attacked at dawn on the 29th of November with three brigades struggling through telegraph wire entanglements which the Federals had stretched between stakes a short distance in front of the ditch.

Tip and his men in camp.
(There is another photo of Tip in the photo section)

In spite of this obstacle the Rebels managed to reach the ditch with relatively light casualties. Longstreet's men did not know that the Highlanders had poured water into the ditch, and while the attack was still forming, the water froze. The Confederates charged the fort and the 79th opened fire. The ground was frozen and covered in sleet which caused the soldiers to lose their footing and fall, slipping and sliding into the ditch where the

Highlanders threw artillery shells with lit fuses. The explosions ripped apart the attackers. Some men did manage to reach the top by climbing on the shoulders of their comrades and were able to place their colors on the parapet. First Sgt. Francis W. Judge of Company K, 79th NY, grabbed the flag of the 51st Georgia and, in spite of a concentrated and deadly fire, was able to return in safety with his trophy into the fort. Judge, was later awarded the Medal of Honor for his action. 813 Rebels were killed while only 9 casualties were suffered by the 79th. Longstreet gave up on Tennessee and joined General Lee's forces in Virginia.

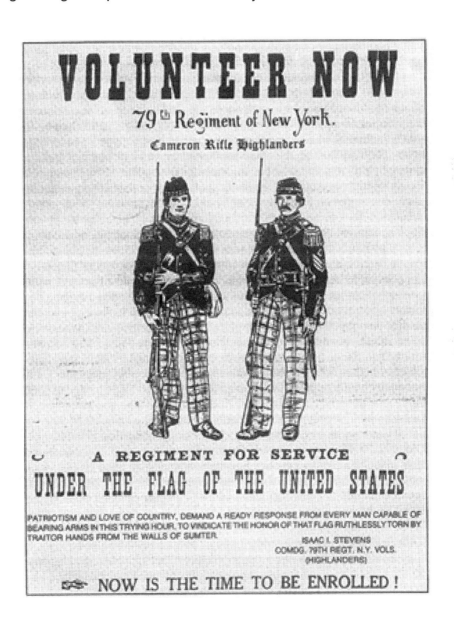

21
General George Custer and Friends

Lieutenant George A. Custer reclining with a dog and fellow staff officers during the Peninsula Campaign.

After General George Custer became chief of cavalry in Texas, he and his wife Libby moved to Austin, where they resided at the Asylum for the Blind. They were acquainted with some wealthy planters, who introduced them to the pleasures of breeding hunting dogs. During the Civil War George Armstrong Custer kept a number of dogs around his headquarters. He loved dogs and horses; he cried in public when one of his favorite dogs died. Though Custer was "as tough, as meticulous, and as professional as any general officer could be" he had never lost the capacity to act like a little boy at times. Selected from about forty of his dogs, he brought along four of his staghounds and was seen with dogs many times. It was not uncommon to see him throwing sticks to them or rolling around in the grass. Brian Dippie said *"Custer was rarely without his dogs. They accompanied him on hunts and on campaigns; they ranged themselves at his feet, rested their heads on his lap, shared his bed and his food, got under foot, made nuisances of themselves, but never lost their special place in his affection. They were like people to him"*. After one engagement, he is also reported to have denied wounded members of his command access to ambulances, which he used instead to transport his hunting dogs.

In a letter to his wife date July 15, 1874 (during the Black Hills expedition) Custer wrote *"As I write, the dogs surround me: "Cardigan" is sleeping on the edge of my bed, "Tuck" at the head, and "Blücher" near by.... "* In another letter dated June 12 1876 : *"Tuck" regularly comes when I am writing, and lays her head on the desk, rooting up my hand with her long nose until I consent to stop and notice her. She and Swift, Lady and Kaiser sleep in my tent."*

One of Custer's dog's. Matida, killed during a buffalo hunt. The general was so broken up about it he wrote this poem to her:

Poor Matida, in life the firmest friend,
The first to welcome, foremost to defend;
Whose honest heart is still your master's own,
Who labors, fights, lives, breathes for him alone.
But who with me shall hold thy former place,
Thine image what new friendship can efface.
Best of thy kind adieu!
The frantic deed which laid thee low
This heart shall ever rue.

When the Battle of Little Bighorn began, Custer let his dogs behind him, but his orderly John Burkman couldn't catch them before they left the pack train and followed their beloved master. Cheyenne warrior Wooden Leg remembered a dog on Custer Hill when the Last Stand had finished. John Burkman said that he had seen one of the dogs on a distant hill, on June 26. None of the dogs has been seen again.

22
Dog Lovers and Friends:
Generals George Pickett, CSA and Rufus Ingalls, US

General George E. Pickett was Rufus Ingalls' frequent guest at Fort Vancouver during the Pig War crisis and they became great friends. Pickett joined the Confederate Army in September 1861 and was promoted to brigadier general in January 1862. Ingalls became chief quartermaster of the Army of the Potomac in September 1861 and was promoted to brigadier general on July 6, 1864. They remained friends even though they ended up on opposite sides of the Civil War.

When Pickett's wife, Sallie, gave birth to their first son, the two armies were encamped facing each other. They often swapped coffee and tobacco under flags of truce. When news of the birth reached the camp, bonfires were lit in celebration all along Pickett's line. When the men of the Union side saw the bonfires they wanted to know what was going on. General Grant sent a few men over to find out why the fires had been lit. When they reported the birth of Pickett's son, Grant said to General Ingalls "Haven't we some kindling on this side of the line? Why don't we strike a light for the young Pickett." In a little while bonfires were flaming from the Federal line. A few days later there was taken through the lines a baby's silver service engraved "To George E. Pickett, Jr from his father's friends U.S. Grant, Rufus Ingalls and George Suckley."

When Grant was President, Pickett and Ingalls together were frequent White House visitors. Ingalls interceded with Grant for Pickett when Pickett was indicted for war crimes. However Pickett's wife, Sallie, (photo below) seemed to have a problem with George's friendship with Ingalls since Ingalls was a Union general. Once when Ingalls came to visit, Sallie was in another room grumbling about having an enemy in her home. She did not know that General Ingalls and her husband were at the door listening. Ingalls said to her "Why, do you know, child, we have slept under the same blanket, fought under the same

flag, eaten out of the same mess pan, dodged the same bullets, scalped the same Indians, made love to the same girls — aye, Pickett, it won't do, by Jove, to tell her all we have done together — no, no— come, shake hands. I am dreadful sorry we have had this terrible kick-up in the family, and all this row and bloodshed, but we are all Americans, damn it, anyhow, and your fellows have been mighty plucky to hold out as they have. Come, that's a good child; shake hands. May I kiss her, Pickett?" Then General Ingalls put into the baby's hands his first greenback.

It is not surprising that Pickett named his favorite dog "Rufus" after his friend. In a letter that he wrote to Sallie while waiting for her to return from a trip, it is obvious that he feels his dog is on the same emotional level as he himself is.

"It is Thursday and the cottage is so empty - so desolate without my darling. Even Rufus feels the absence of his beautiful mistress and a few minutes ago, to show his sympathy for his lonesome master, brought and laid on my knee a little slipper which, if I did not know it belonged to my own fairy princess, would make me think that another Cinderella with a tinier foot had also forgotten the midnight hour. I gave no evidence of my appreciation of his effort to comfort me and Rufus trotted off and brought me the other slipper. "Good dog," I said, "good dog," patting him on the head. Then fondling the little slippers and putting them beside me I took up my pencil and pad to tell you all about it. Presently, looking around, I saw Rufus planning to bring me everything in the room belonging to you. He has a lot of dog sense and I tried to make him understand that the slippers had been sufficiently effective in consoling me, but he would not be convinced until I whistled our song, "Believe me, if all those endearing young charms." Then trying to howl an accompaniment and failing, he wagged his tail, lay down at my feet and went to sleep. Every day when I come in to dinner he trots up in front of your picture and barks till I take it down, then looking down at it barks again, while I encourage him, saying, "Tell her all about it, old man; tell her all about it." When he has told you about it he lies down beside it, his paw on the frame, wagging his tail and looking up at me till he thinks I have shown sufficient appreciation of his admiration and devotion to you, and then he jumps up and points and barks at the place on the rack from which it was taken until it is duly kissed and replaced. Oh, he's a great dog, little one, and great company for me, but both he and I and everything else are lonesome for you and we have promised our souls that when you come back we will vie with each other in our efforts to make you happy."

It is quite apparent that both men had a special love for their canine companions. Not much was written about General Ingalls' dog; however, it appears the general was very fond of having his Dalmatian appear in photographs. Photography was still in it's infancy during this time so it was uncommon for someone to have so many photos of a pet. A few of those photos are shown here.

General Ingalls with family (above) and driving the wagon.
Photo on opposite page is general Ingalls' horse

23
General William Barksdale's Mourning Dog

Confederate General William Barksdale led his Mississippi boys into battle at Gettysburg. . Barksdale was wounded in his left knee, followed by a cannonball to his left foot, and finally was hit by another bullet to his chest, knocking him off his horse. He told his aide, W.R. Boyd, "I am killed! Tell my wife and children that I died fighting at my post." His troops were forced to leave him for dead on the field and he died the next morning in a Union field hospital (the Joseph Hummelbaugh farmhouse) and was buried there. His wife traveled to Gettysburg to exhume her husband's remains. She wanted to return to their home in Mississippi and bury her husband there. She took the General's favorite hunting dog along on her trip. It was a trip that broke the heart of Barksdale's dog. As the old dog was led to his master's grave, he fell down onto the ground and began to howl. No matter what Mrs. Barksdale did, she was unable to pull the animal away even though the General's remains had already been loaded onto a wagon. Realizing there was nothing more she could do to persuade the dog to come with her, she started the trip home. For days afterward, the loyal dog refused to budge and turned down all offers of food and water from the local s of Gettysburg. Many people tried to lure the dog away and offer him a new home. He eventually died on his master's former grave.

24
Calamity, 28th Regiment Wisconsin Volunteers

The 28th marched from Little Rock to Pine Bluff, Arkansas the first week of November 1863, and were stationed there one year. Soon after arriving at Pine Bluff a small puppy dog was found by Peter Bodett, (right) a member of Co. B, 28th Wis. Vols. It grew to be a fair sized dog, was black on back and sides, and yellow underneath. In the summer of 1864 as Capt. Thomas N. Stevens was riding by the barrack just at daylight the dog ran out and barked at the horse and the Capt was nearly thrown from the saddle, he drew his revolver and fired three shots at the dog and two of them wounded him. As the dog was quite a favorite in the Regiment word of his being wounded soon spread and Col E. B.

Gray commanding the Regiment named him Calamity. The dog recovered from his wounds and was always called Calamity. The dog became very useful in the Regiment and would go out with the forage train and often catch a hog by the ear and hold it until the Soldiers could kill it as they were not allowed to shoot at it. This dog became known in the whole Brigade during the last year of the war. The Regiment was sent from Mobile, Alabama, to Texas the first of June 1865, and started for home from Brownsville, Texas, the last of August.

25
Emiline Pigott and her Spy Dog

Throughout the Civil War, many of the spies well-to-do white women. Women spying for either the North or the South used their large hoop skirts to hide weapons, secret documents and other contraband.

Emeline Pigott (left) was born and raised in Harlowe Township in Carteret County, North Carolina. When she was twenty-five she moved with her family to Crab Point, on the North Carolina coast. Their farm was just across the creek from where soldiers of the 26th North Carolina were stationed to defend the coast. She helped the sick and wounded soldiers, even bringing some to her home to nurse. She also collected mail from the soldiers and left food, clothing, medicine, and other items in hollow trees for the rebels to pick up later. She hosted socials for Union soldiers and local fishermen during which these parties provided valuable intelligence concerning Federal military and naval installations. During this time she would gather critical information. Wearing a hoop skirt she would sometimes carry as much as thirty pounds of supplies and intelligence information. One day Gen. Pierre Gustave T. Beauregard (right) had been eagerly awaiting information regarding Union troop movements and positions. When Emiline arrived with her pet dog, General Beauregard petted the dog affectionately. He was a fat dog with coarse and springy fur and he wagged his tail when the general petted him. Emiline said to the General, "I have the report with me but it was hard to get it through Union lines. Once I was stopped and they searched me thoroughly." Then she asked the general to borrow his knife

and Beauregard watched in shock as she bent over her little pet and plunged the knife into the dog's side. The General was horrified, but then he noticed the dog was still wagging its tail. Emiline kept sawing then removed the fake fur skin she had sewn around the dog's middle and handed Gen. Beauregard the report ingeniously hidden underneath the dog's second coat of fur.

In 1865 while conducting her normal activities, she was arrested and jailed. While officials were looking for someone to search the lady, Emeline chewed and swallowed some incriminating information, but much information was still located hidden in her hoop skirt. She was sent to New Bern where she was imprisoned. She was convicted and sentenced to death. Though she faced the death penalty, she was inexplicably released. She was, however, watched and harassed until the end of the war. Up until the day she died in 1916 she would never reveal how she came to be released from prison.

26
Dick the Four Footed Orderly

Reprinted from The Pictorial Book of Anecdotes and Incidents of the War of the Rebellion By Richard Miller Devens 1867

As we were flying about in every direction, now here, now there, says a pleasing writer and eye witness of what is here narrated, with a pad for one, a basin and sponge to wet the wounds of another, cologne for a third, and milk punch for a fourth, I felt Dick, our hospital dog my faithful friend and ally a four footed Vidocq, in his mode of scenting out grievances, seize my dress in his teeth, pull it hard and look eagerly up in my face. "What is it Dick? I am too busy to attend to you just now". Another hard pull and a beseeching look in his eyes. "Presently my fine fellow, presently. Gettysburg men must come first.". He wags his tail furiously and still pulls my dress. Does he mean that he wants me for one of them? Perhaps so. "Come, Dick, I'll go with you." He starts off delighted, leads me to the ward where those worst wounded have been placed, travels the whole length of it to the upper corner where lies a man apparently badly wounded and crying like a child. I had seen him brought in on a stretcher but in the confusion had not noticed where he had been taken. Dick halted as we arrived at the bed, looked at me, as much as to say "There! Isn't that a case requiring attention?" and then as though quite satisfied to resign him into my hands, trotted quietly off. He did not notice my approach. I therefore stood watching him a little while. His arm and hand from which the bandage had partially slipped were terribly swollen, the wound was in the wrist (or rather as I afterwards found the ball had entered the palm of his hand and had come out at his wrist) and appeared to be as it subsequently proved a very severe one. My boast that I could make a pretty good conjecture what state a man came from by looking at him did not avail me here. I was utterly at fault. His fair hair, Saxon face, so far as I could judge of it, as he lay sobbing on his pillow had something feminine almost child like in the innocence and gentleness of its expression, and my first thought was one which has constantly recurred on acquaintance "How utterly unfit for soldier!" He wanted the quick energy of the New Englander who when badly wounded rarely fails to his origin. He had none of the rough offhand dash of our Western brothers; could never have had it even in health …nor yet the stolidity of our PA Germans. No it was clear that must wait until he chose to enlighten me as to his home. After a few minutes study, I was convinced that his tears were not from the pain of his wound, there was no contraction of the brow, no tension of the muscles, no quivering of the frame… he seemed simply very weary, very languid, like a tired child, and I resolved to act accordingly. "I have been so busy with our defenders this afternoon" said "I that I have bad no time to come and thank you." He started raised his tear stained face and said with a wondering air "To thank me for what?" " For what" said I "Haven't you been keeping the rebels away from us? Don't you know that if it hadn't been for you and many like you we might at this moment have been flying from our homes and General Lee and his men occupying our city? You don't seem to know how grateful we are to you. We feel as though we could never do enough for our brave Gettysburg men to return what they have done for us "This seemed quite a novel idea and the tears were stopped to muse upon it. "We tried to do our duty ma'am I know that" " I know it too and I think I could make a pretty good guess what corps you belong to. Suppose I try. Wasn't it the Second corps? You look to me like one of General Hancock's men. You know they were praised in the papers for their bravery. Am I right?" The poor tired face brightened instantly. The random shot had hit the mark. "Yes, Second Corps. Do you know by my cap?" "Your cap? You don t wear your cap in bed do you? I haven't seen your cap. I guessed by that wound. It must have been made where there was pretty hard fighting and I knew the Second Corps had done their share of that." But this was dangerous ground as I felt the moment the allusion to his wound was made, the sympathy was too direct.. and his eyes filled at once. Seeing my mistake I plunged off rapidly on tack "Did you notice my assistant who came in with me just now? He"s been over to see you before for he and told me you wanted me" "I wanted you! No ma'am that's mistake. No one's been near me since bathed me and gave me clean clothes. I know there hasn't for I watched running all about but none came to me and I want so much to have my arm dressed." And the ready tears at once began to flow. "There is no mistake. I told you my assistant orderly came to me in the ladies room and told me that you needed me. Think again who has been since you were brought in.?" "Not a single soul ma'am indeed, not a thing but a dog standing looking in my face and wagging his tail as if he was pitying me." "But a dog exactly, he's my assistant orderly he came over to me pulled my dress and wouldn't rest till I came see you. I am surprised you speak slightingly of poor Dick." Here was at once a safe and fertile theme. I entered at large upon merits, his fondness for the men, greater fondness occasionally for their dinners- his having made way with three lunches just prepared for the men who were starting- the result probably of having heard the old story that the surgeons eat what is intended for the men, our finding him one day on our table with his head in the pitcher of lemonade, and how I tried to explain to him that such was not the way of proving his regards for his friends the soldiers, but I feared without much effect. In short I made a long story out of nothing till the ward master arrived with his supper saying that the doctor's orders were that the new cases should all take something to eat before he examined their wounds. My friend had quite forgotten his own troubles in listening to Dick's varied talents and allowed me to give him his supper very quietly. As I found he was really too much exhausted even to raise his uninjured arm to his mouth I had the pleasure of seeing him smile for good bye.

27
Modern Dogs of War

Thousands of dogs have served our nation's military and have died in action. Over 2000 dogs died in World War I. At the end of the Vietnam War, our military left most of the American war dogs there, approximately 2800 of the 3000 who served. The Army Quartermaster Corps officially began the U.S. Armed Forces first war dog training during WWII. By 1945 they had trained almost 10,000 war dogs for the Army, Navy, Marine Corps and Coast Guard. Fifteen War Dog platoons served overseas in World War II. Seven saw service in Europe and eight in the Pacific. In 1951, the responsibility for training military dogs was given to the Military Police Corps. Dogs continued to serve the armed forces with distinction in Korea, Vietnam, Desert Storm, Afghanistan and Iraq and many recent contingency operations. Military working dogs have served without compensation or recognition, nor been honored for their sacrifice. We owe it to ourselves to remember those faithful creatures that served with, protected, and fought beside our men and women, and whose countless deeds saved so many American lives and helped protect our freedom. Yes, we remember, we need to remember man's best friend and we owe it to these unsung warriors to never forget. The dogs listed here are only a few.

U.S. Marine Corps Sgt. Jose R. Zepeda, (left) attached to Task Force, 2nd Battalion, 7th Marine Regiment, rests with his military working dog Jaycee in Zaidon, Iraq, March 24, 2007, during a search for weapons and insurgent activity. Photo by Cpl. Samuel D. Corum Courtesy of U.S. Marine Corps

Left: Zeko, an explosive detection canine, takes a breather, after his handler puts on his specially made ballistic "doggles", used to protect the eyes from heat and blowing sand, and bullet proof vest for his daily training at the newly built training course located at Forward Operating Base McHenry, Iraq. Photo by Spc. Barbara Ospina Courtesy of the United States Army.

Right: U.S. Army Spc. Dennis Bechtel, a dog handler attached to 10th Mountain Division, and his working dog, Randy, sniff cracks in a 30 foot high man made hole for weapon caches outside the village of Uch Tapa, Iraq, during a cordon and search mission Dec. 31, 2007. U.S. Air Force photo by Staff Sgt. Samuel Bendet.

U.S. Army Sgt. 1st Class Randy Knight, a crew chief with Charlie Company, 1st Battalion, 52nd Aviation Regiment, hoists Meki, an Air Force military working dog, up to a medical evacuation helicopter during training at Fort Wainwright July 23, 2007. U.S. Army photo by Staff Sgt. Matthew T. MacRoberts

STUBBY, Bull Terrier mix, WWI. The most decorated war dog in U.S. history. His stuffed remains, ashes, and medals are currently stored in a packing crate in a storage room of the National Museum of American History, which considers the dog an "oddity with little educational merit."

NORMAN SADLER, Fox Terrier, fundraiser during WWII.

BOOTS, trick dog, fundraiser during WWII.

RONNIE, German Shepherd, WWII, U.S. Coast Guard Dog Patrol.

BOB, Collie mix, WWII, led more forays into German territory than any other U.S. soldier in WWII, human or canine.

BUSTER, WWII, killed in action.

RICKY, Welsh Shepherd, parachuting scout dog, WWII.

DUKE, Doberman Pinscher, served in the Pacific during WWII.

CHIPS, German Shepherd-Collie-Husky mix, WWII, Tank guard dog and the most decorated dog in WWII being awarded the Silver Star for Valor and a Purple Heart. When he and his handler were attacked by a concealed machine gun in July 1943 during the invasion of Sicily, he streaked for the Italian machine gun pillbox, capturing 4 Italian soldiers and saving his handler. He suffered powder burns and a scalp wound - proof that the Italians had tried to kill him. That same night he helped capture another 10 Italian soldiers. The U.S. newspapers called him a hero. General Eisenhower personally thanked him for his services. Chips' military honors were removed because the commander of the Order of the Purple Heart determined that decorating a dog was "...demeaning to servicemen."

DUG, Belgian Shepherd, Korean War.

BRUTE, Belgian Shepherd, Korean War.

ROY, Belgian Shepherd, Korean War.

SHERI, Belgian Shepherd, Korean War.

SARGE 1A43, German Shepherd, Vietnam.

PRINCE 55-M-9, German Shepherd mix, Vietnam.

LUKE, black Labrador Retriever, Vietnam

PATCHES, Vietnam, one of the few war dogs given passage back home to the United States.

NEMO, German Shepherd, Depsite losing an eye to gunfire, he threw himself on 4 Viet Cong to save his handler in 1966. Both survived. one of the few war dogs given passage back home to the United States.

MAC, first canine casualty in Vietnam.

PAL, scout dog, Vietnam.

TROUBLES, scout dog, Vietnam.

VALENTINE 3F38, German Shepherd, died in Vietnam.

BUCK, German Shepherd mix, Vietnam, killed in action.

ROYAL 19X8, German Shepherd, Vietnam, killed in action.

DUKE 383M, German Shepherd, Vietnam, killed in action.

CLACKER, German Shepherd, Vietnam, killed in action.
KREIGER, German Shepherd, Vietnam, killed in action.
PONCHO, German Shepherd, Vietnam, killed in action.
DUKE 645f, German Shepherd, Vietnam, missing in action.
EBONY, German Shepherd, Vietnam, 47th Scout Dog Platoon.
DUFFER, German Shepherd, Vietnam, 212th Sentry Dog Co.
SUZIE, German Shepherd, Vietnam. Her handler gave her his Bronze Star.
BLACKIE 129X, left behind in Vietnam.
HEIDI, scout dog, left behind in Vietnam.
KRISTIANNA, German Shepherd, left behind in Vietnam.
WARRIOR, German Shepherd, left behind in Vietnam.
COMMANDER, German Shepherd, left behind in Vietnam.
WINSTON, German Shepherd, left behind in Vietnam.
TIMBER, German Shepherd, left behind in Vietnam.
CLIPPER, German Shepherd, left behind in Vietnam.
ORION, German Shepherd, left behind in Vietnam.
SMOKEY, German Shepherd, nicknamed "Flop," left behind in Vietnam.
REX, German Shepherd, nicknamed "Punky," Vietnam.
YORK, German Shepherd, Vietnam.
DUKE, German Shepherd, Vietnam.
BOY, German Shepherd, Vietnam.
NASTY, German Shepherd, Vietnam.
ZORRO, German Shepherd, Vietnam.
MAX, German Shepherd, Vietnam.
KOENIG, German Shepherd, Vietnam.
BRIAN-4M4, German Shepherd, Vietnam.
KING, German Shepherd, Vietnam.
KIESER, German Shepherd, Vietnam
HUDSONS KING, German Shepherd, Vietnam.
RUSTY 775E, German Shepherd, Vietnam.
IRKO, German Shepherd, Vietnam.
TIGER, German Shepherd, Vietnam.
INK, German Shepherd, Vietnam.
REBEL, German Shepherd, Vietnam.
CHIEF, German Shepherd, Vietnam.
SMOKIE 6X65, German Shepherd, Vietnam.
SLIM SN# 84M6, German Shepherd, Vietnam.
PUDDLES 807M, German Shepherd, Vietnam.
BRUISER, German Shepherd, Vietnam.
ROGER 3M84, German Shepherd, Vietnam.
DUKE 847A, German Shepherd, Vietnam.

BUDDY A601, German Shepherd, Vietnam.
BIG BOY, German Shepherd, Vietnam.
TARZAN W195, German Shepherd, Vietnam.
BLITZ, German Shepherd, Vietnam.
MACK, German Shepherd, Vietnam.
ERIC, German Shepherd, Vietnam.
FRITZ 584F, German Shepherd, Vietnam.
GEISHA A871, German Shepherd, Vietnam.
REX 75M3, German Shepherd, Vietnam.
SHEPPY, German Shepherd, Vietnam.
CLYDE, German Shepherd, Vietnam.
CHEROKEE, German Shepherd, Vietnam.
SPOOK 235X, German Shepherd, Vietnam.
BUFFY 87M3, German Shepherd, Vietnam.
KNIGHT, German Shepherd, Vietnam.
LISLE, German Shepherd-Collie mix, served the U.S. Army in the early 1980's.
THOR, German Shepherd, Desert Storm.
BUNS, German Shepherd, Desert Storm.
SMOKEY, German Shepherd, Desert Storm.
BANDIT, German Shepherd, Desert Storm.
ASTOR, German Shepherd, Desert Storm.
PENNY, Beagle, Desert Storm.
TOSCA, Belgian Malinois, Desert Storm.
NERO 304J, Belgian Malinois, Desert Storm.
CARLO, Belgian Malinois, Desert Storm.
During a ceremony in which Carlo's handler received the Bronze Star for his service in Kuwait, his handler removed the medal from his own uniform and pinned it onto Carlo's collar, saying, "Carlo worked harder than me. He was always in front of me."
COOPER, Yellow Lab, Operation Iraqi Freedom, 94th Mine Dog Detachment on July 6, 2007, 20 year old Cpl. Kory Wiens and Cooper were killed by an explosive device after less than a year of service. They were buried together.

Civil War Photos

This dog is saying
"I am the dog that went through the army with the 25th Iowa Infantry"

Officers and a lady at headquarters of 1st Brigade, Horse Artillery
Brandy Station, Va. Feb. 1864

General George Stoneman seated right and General Henry M Naglee seated third from left with members of their staffs.

Fair Oaks, Virginia (vicinity). Gen. George Stoneman and staff

Bermuda Hundred Virginia Officers by their quarters near the signal tower

Company M, 9th New York Heavy Artillery, in a fort August, 1865

**Company K,
3d Regiment
Massachusetts Heavy
Artillery at Fort Stevens
August, 1865**

**Officers and men of
Company F,
3d Massachusetts Heavy
Artillery,
in Fort Stevens August,
1865**

22nd New York State Militia with their tiny friend,
near Harpers Ferry, Virginia,1861.

Here is another photo of the Cameron Highlanders with their dog, Tip.

District of Columbia. Gen. William Gamble and staff at Camp Stoneman, the cavalry depot at Giesborough Point May, 1865

164th New York Infantry. Taken between 1861 and 1865. The two soldiers sitting on the right have a white dog between them.

Photograph from the main eastern theater of war, the siege of Petersburg, Virginia

81

Petersburg, Virginia, commissary department, 50th New York Engineers

**7th New York State Militia,
Camp Cameron,
Washington D.C., 1861**

**Band of
9th Veteran Reserve Corps
Washington, D.C.**

84

**Washington, D. C. 9th U.S. Veteran Reserve Corps
(Regimental band shown in front)**

9th US Veteran Reserve Barracks Washington, 1865

**General Napoleon Bonaparte McLaughlen and staff near
Washington, D.C. July, 1895**

The photograph was taken after the Civil War. General George A. Custer is pictured on the plains, with Indian Scouts. He is shown in camp with his dogs. Custer was often pictured with dogs nearby.

This image shows the crewmembers of the *USS Hunchback*, including one sailor (to the right of the cannon), who is shown holding a white dog.

Officers of the *USS Miami*, including one shown holding his hunting rifle and bag, with his two dogs at his feet. The officer at left has a little dog resting on his arm

Group of Co. A, 8th New York State Militia with their dog in Arlington, Virginia, June, 1861

USS Patapsco (1862)

Unidentified Sailors– Possibly aboard the USS Patapsco

Gen. Daniel White and staff, 1865

Operators of military telegraph. Richmond, Virginia, June 1865.

References

The Pictorial Book of Anecdotes and Incidents of the War of the Rebellion
by Richard Miller Devens 1884

1862 The Army of the Southwest and the First Campaign in Arkansas Annals of Iowa, April, 1868.
Iowa State Historical Society

Thank God Lincoln Had Only One 79th Highlander Regiment
By Tony Mandara

The Seventy-ninth Highlanders, New York Volunteers in the War of Rebellion
By William Todd 1886

New York in the War of the Rebellion, 3rd ed.
by Frederick Phisterer 1912.

History of the Third Regiment of Wisconsin Veteran Volunteer Infantry
By Edwin Eustace Bryant 1891

The Rebellion Record: A Diary of American Events
By Frank Moore

Military History and Reminiscences of the Thirteenth Regiment of Illinois Volunteer Infantry in the Civil War in the United States, 1861-1865
By Illinois Infantry 13th regt.

Calamity, A Dog Soldier of the 28th Wisconsin
by Sgt. Lauren S. Barker, Company A

The Little Mascot
by James I. Robertson Jr.

The 91st Pennsylvania Volunteer Infantry
Rootsweb.com

Massillon Museum Looks at the Civil War
by Gary Brown

Antietam: The Soldiers' Battle
by John M. Priest

Harvey, the Yankee War Dog
By Timothy R Brooks

Dogs of War: And Stories of Other Beasts of Battle in the Civil War
by Marilyn Seguin

History of Pennsylvania Volunteers 1861-1865 Ninety-first Regiment vol 3
By Samuel Penniman Bates

91st PA Regiment Company C, descriptive roll, number 11 (William H Brown)

1860 US census, Pennsylvania, Philadelphia, Philadelphia city, ward 2, page 198 [handwritten and stamped], lines 35-40 (William H Brown)

Biographical Directory Of The American Congress 1774-1949,
85th Cong., 2nd sess. U.S. Congress. House. H. Doc. 607
Washington, D.C.: U.S. Government Printing Office, 1950

Field, Fort and Fleet; Being a Series of Brilliant and Authentic Sketches of the Most Notable Battles of the Late Civil War
By M. Quad 1885

Lee's Last Major General: Bryan Grimes of North Carolina
by T. Harrell Allen

Sketches of My Life
By Charlotte Emily Bryan Grimes

Touched by Fire. The Life, Death and Mythic Afterlife of George Armstrong Custer.
By L. Barnett 1996

My Life on the Plains: Or Personal Experiences
by George Armstrong Custer

George W. Alexander and Castle Thunder: A Confederate Prison and Its Commandant
By Frances H. Casstevens 2004

Pickett and His Men
By La Salle Corbell Pickett

The Heart of a Soldier: As Revealed in the Intimate Letters of General George Pickett
by Seth Moyle

Portals to Hell - Mechanicsburg, PA
by Lonnie Speer 1997

Curly's War Record - A Dog Which Deserved a Pension from Uncle Sam for His Service With the 11th Ohio Volunteer Infantry
By: T.L. Stewart, Co. A, Eleventh Ohio Volunteer Infantry

Battle of Little Bighorn
by Mary Trotter Kion

Antietam: The Soldiers' Battle, A history of the famous Iron Brigade
by John M. Priest

Gettysburg
by Stephen W. Sears

Civil War Memories of Robert C. Carden
by Robert C. Carden, Company B, 16th Tennessee Infantry 1912

The Civil War in Song and Story: 1860-1865
By Frank Moore 1889

The Intelligence of Dogs
By Dr. Stanley Coren

The Journal of Surgeon Samuel P. Boyer (The entry dated March 11, 1863)

Most Devoted Friend - Iron Brigade Sixth Wisconsin Captain Werner Von Bachelle
Major Rufus Dawes

Newspapers & Periodicals

The Richmond Whig
May 1,1865

The Richmond Whig
May 19, 1865

The New York Times
May 24,1865

The Libby Chronicle
August 28, 1863

The Ohio Soldier
May 5, 1888
Saturday Evening Post
December 27, 1862

The Philadelphia Inquirer
December 19, 1862

Murfreesboro Post
Mon, Feb 4, 2008
Dogs Were Spies by Shirley Farris Jones

Harper's Weekly
November 8, 1862
Union Jack, The Pet of our Richmond Prisoners

Harper's Weekly
June 25, 1864
The Dog of the Regiment

Northwest Arkansas Times
Sunday, July 2, 2006
Headquarters House ties modern Fayetteville to Civil War Past
By Drew Terry

ACWS Newsletter
June, 1998

Gettysburg Compiler
January 12, 1863
Singular Fidelity of a Dog on the Battlefield

Confederate Veteran
Vol. XVII, No. 4, April 1909

The Delta General
Volume 9 Issue 10 September 2007

The Missouri Review
Volume 24, Number 2, 2001

The Old Liner Newsletter

Panabasis Journal of the Janus Museum
December 2005

The official blog of writer and historian Dale Cox

Images

The Library of Congress;
Prints & Photographs Division; Prints & Photographs Catalog;
Civil War Photographs 1861 – 1865

National Archives and Records Administration
Washington, DC 20408

United States Department of Defense

Wikimedia Commons
Public Domain Civil War Images
commons.wikimedia.org/

Maps on front and back cover by Robert Knox Sneden (1823 – 1918)

Cover Design by A. Palagruto

Made in the USA
Lexington, KY
26 January 2012